D0794187

Published in Nashville, Tennessee, by Rutledge Hill
Press®, 211 Seventh Avenue North, Nashville,
Tennessee 37219.

Distributed in Canada by H. B. Fenn & Company, Ltd.,
34 Nixon Road, Bolton, Ontario L7E 1W2.

Distributed in Australia by The Five Mile Press Pty.,
Ltd., 22 Summit Road, Noble Park, Victoria 3174.

Distributed in New Zealand by Southern Publishers
Group, 22 Burleigh Street, Grafton, Auckland.

Distributed in the United Kingdom by Verulam
Publishing, Ltd., 152a Park Street Lane, Park Street, St.
Albans, Hertfordshire AL2 2AU.

Typography by Compass Communications, Inc.,
Nashville, Tennessee

Library of Congress Cataloging-in-Publication Data
is available.

ISBN: 1-55853-740-6

Printed in Hong Kong

1 2 3 4 5 6 7 8 9–03 02 01 00 99

INTRODUCTION

I earn my living as an author and inspirational speaker. My profession has allowed me to visit with, and learn from, thousands of people from all walks of life—from those who earn minimum wage to others making millions. Sadly, as I reflect on what I have learned from this laboratory of life, I have come to a sobering conclusion: We live in a country with the highest standard of living but the lowest quality of life in history! People's minds are full but their hearts are empty.

Amid the chaos of today's high-tech society, many people are searching for their identity. Others are looking for happiness or for the true meaning in life. In this ultra-competitive and rapidly changing world, many people are left wondering if they can truly make a difference. You can! The purpose of this book is to share what I believe are powerful motivational tips and ideas that will inspire you to go out and make a difference, just like a close friend of mine, Kenneth Tedford, did.

Kenneth told me the story of how, as a young boy, he was declared "mentally retarded." His alcoholic mother died when he was eight, and while his adoptive mother loved him, his adoptive father was embarrassed to have Kenny around. One day during class in grade school, the teacher asked students to draw stick figures depicting what they wanted to be when they grew up. While other students produced renderings of firemen, nurses, and policemen, Kenny drew a stick man standing next to a podium, with the American flag in the background. When Kenny explained that he wanted to be a motivational speaker and make people feel good, the teacher retorted, "But Kenny, you know you can't do that. You're retarded." Kenny responded by saying, "Well, you're a teacher and you're not real smart!"

The teacher took Kenny to the principal's office for punishment and explained to the principal what had happened. After the teacher left, the principal got down on one knee, looked straight into Kenny's eyes, and said, "Kenny, that teacher is a very cruel person, and I know that you can be whatever you dream to be." A series of tests later found Kenny to be hearing impaired, not retarded. He went on to become a motivational speaker, a standup comedian, and an author of several children's books.

The goal of this book is to inspire you to keep on keeping on, to free yourself of the dysfunctional junk pulling you down, and to again learn how to soar—just like Kenny did. I believe every American, and every citizen of the world for that matter, has it within himself or herself to run the race embodying higher ideals and establishing the highest of goals. May the entries in this book touch your heart and soul and serve to brighten your path as you join me on this inspirational journey of hope, freedom, and excellence.

THE POCKET POWER BOOK OF MOTIVATION

GREATNESS AWAITS THOSE WHO DARE TO SOAR.

Successful people do what
unsuccessful people won't.

Develop a sense of
urgency to the task at
hand, and pay attention to
the details.

Stand for what is right,
even if it means you stand
alone.

We achieve what we
believe.

LIFE'S CHALLENGES ARE NO MATCH FOR THE WILL OF THE HUMAN SPIRIT.

Start today with a renewed commitment to excellence, and anticipate success.

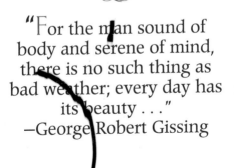

"For the man sound of body and serene of mind, there is no such thing as bad weather; every day has its beauty . . ."
—George Robert Gissing

Keep your eyes on the stars.

LIFE: **Live It Fully Everyday.**

A negative attitude cancels out positive skills.

Be willing to step outside "the comfort zone."

The mind's attitude determines life's altitude.

Are you becoming complacent?

Surround yourself with dream makers, not dream killers.

Thought should always
precede action.

Don't spend too much
time in thought, as action
produces greatness.

You must believe that you
are the *power of one.*

Listen to the internal
impulse to soar.

Potential is one of
life's greatest gifts–don't
waste it.

What you stand for is
what you will become.

You must have the
courage to live what
others only dream.

Believe in yourself–doubt
leads to defeat.

Passion: the high-performance fuel of life.

Forget the failures of the past and embrace the promises of the future.

DARE TO BE DIFFERENT!

Work harder and smarter.

Resolve today to make the
best use of tomorrow.

Have fun and celebrate
your successes!

We rise to greatness by lifting others.

The only limits to life's opportunities are the ones you set.

Always see the glass as
half-full!

Make sure the mission is
honorable.

THE WINNING EDGE IS A DAILY COMMITMENT TO INDIVIDUAL IMPROVEMENT.

Passion, Courage,
Commitment—This is life!

Today is the first day of
the rest of your life.

Positive thoughts are
fertilizer for the mind.

A passionate belief in the
mission will yield
extraordinary results.

Goals are thoughts put
into action.

Freedom is a gift—open it
every day.

How you feel on the inside directly affects how you perform on the outside.

A healthy diet will energize you for the long haul.

Seek advice from
successful people.

Think of setbacks as new
opportunities to excel.

Daydreams are thoughts
without action.

ACHIEVEMENT IS
IMPOSSIBLE
WITHOUT CHANGE.

Life without movement is
death.

The true riches of life
come naturally as we
enrich the lives of others.

Life is lived by learning
from the past and soaring
into the future.

"THE SOUL NEVER
THINKS WITHOUT
A PICTURE."
—Aristotle

Faith in God gives you the
eternal security that frees
you to succeed.

PEOPLE: **P**eople **E**xpect
Openness, **P**assion, **L**ove,
and **E**xcellence.

Our challenge is to take our talents to their highest level.

Emulate the habits of the winners, not the also-rans.

CHOOSE PERFORMANCE OVER CONFORMANCE.

God has faith in you,
and He is waiting for you
to do the impossible to
please Him.

Read *Strive to Excel:
The Will and Wisdom of
Vince Lombardi.*

Why wait for tomorrow
when we can start
changing the world today?

"We must learn to live by
our enthusiasm."
—Woodrow Wilson

Never put yourself into a place too small to grow.

Strive to make yourself and your organization No. 1.

Better to create
a future we love
than to endure
one we don't.

Set goals and modify your
actions accordingly.

Take an active role in
helping your community.

Make time and take time
to recharge your batteries.

Creativity is an unlimited power source when you learn how to harness it.

Look at life through the windshield, not the rear-view mirror.

Better to be good at something you love than to be great at something you don't.

Tell five people over the next week how much you appreciate them.

CLIMB HIGH,
CLIMB FAR.

No one needs a smile so much as those who have none left to give.

∞

We are the only limitations to our faith.

∞

"How can one consent to creep when one feels an impulse to soar?"
—Helen Keller

Success occurs when
preparation meets
opportunity.

The heart cannot seek the
future if the mind is mired
in the past.

Why mingle with
mediocrity when you can
soar with excellence?

The next time you critique
someone's performance,
offer him or her at least as
many praises as criticisms.

BLAZE YOUR OWN
TRAIL—DON'T WAIT
FOR OTHERS TO
CLEAR THE PATH.

Courage is not the
absence of fear but acting
in the face of it.

If inspiration is the fuel,
hope is the spark that
ignites the heart's passion.

Take some time to smell
the roses–then move on.

Life is not what you are
living *with* but what you
are living *for.*

Life is a race–finish strong!

THE QUESTION IS
NOT WHETHER YOU
ARE MAKING A
LIVING, BUT
WHETHER YOU ARE
MAKING A LIFE.

Success is waking up in
the morning with
someplace to go.

Life's greatest obstacle is
not failure but the fear of
failure.

We truly fail only when we
stop trying.

Life's most powerful combination: A passionate heart driven by a positive attitude.

Watch *Rocky* and *Steel Magnolias* again.

Success is found on the far side of "good enough."

PERSISTENCE IS AN ENTHUSIASTIC RESPONSE TO FAILURE.

Reward others for "your" successes.

"It is the nature of man to rise to greatness if greatness is expected of him."
–John Steinbeck

Compile a list of a dozen things you want to do or places to go before you die, and get started!

Idle time means you're not moving forward.

Aim high. You usually hit what you aim for.

Each failure gets you one step closer to success.

Be aggressive, but not oppressive!

GREAT ACHIEVERS ARE ORDINARY PEOPLE WITH EXTRAORDINARY AMBITION.

Failure is the path of least persistence.

There's always another way around or over the mountain.

Freedom is the pursuit of spiritual significance.

If you're not changing,
you're not in first place.

Worry is crabgrass of
the soul.

The future is in your
hands.

Don't catch the paralysis
of perfection.

"When you're not
practicing, someone
somewhere is, and when
you meet they will win."
—Senator Bill Bradley

Many things in life will catch your eye, but only a few will catch your heart. Pursue those.

Each day you get better or worse–it's your choice.

Push yourself. Only you can motivate you.

God has given you another day; rejoice and be thankful.

Motivation is what turns knowledge and skill into success.

Losers fear success and prosperity.

"One man with courage
makes a majority."
—Thomas Jefferson

Success is
High-touch, not
High-tech.

Life's most honorable
mission: living above the
level of mediocrity.

You must break the chains
of the past to experience
the freedom of the future.

There is no replacement
for effort.

Attitudes are contagious.
Is yours worth catching?

Always tell the truth.

"To accomplish great
things we must not only
act, but also dream; not
only plan, but also believe."
—Anatole France

DON'T JUST TALK
ABOUT IT. DO IT!

Exceed others'
expectations of you—even
your own.

"Climb not for the peak
you see, but the one
concealed to thee."
—Jesse Owens

Life is excellence, and the pursuit of excellence is life.

Feigning confidence in a stressful situation isn't a bad way to start.

Exercise mind over muscle.

When we tolerate what
others celebrate, we
ultimately will celebrate
what we tolerate.

There is passion in
togetherness.

The problems of the world
are no match for the power
of the human spirit.

Life's greatest challenge is
the pursuit of potential.

Even though you are only
one, you are never alone.

Well-treated employees
produce great results.

YOUR CHARACTER
WILL ULTIMATELY
DETERMINE YOUR
DESTINY.

It's a dream until you
write it down; then it
becomes a goal.

Walk a mile outdoors
every other day and be
reinvigorated by the
fresh air.

Letting God means
letting go.

Never doubt that a group
of sharing, caring, and
serving people can achieve
the impossible.

Don't quit before the blessing.

Deliver the goods.

Praise a job well done.

I don't care how much you know; I just want to know how much you care.

M.B.A.: **M**op **B**ucket
Attitude

Preparation beats pride
nine times out of ten!

Seek out the answers
before you're asked the
questions.

OUTHUSTLE YOUR COMPETITION.

Answer the door when opportunity knocks.

Life is a gift: Enjoy it deeply, learn from it daily, and use it wisely.

Excellence is not optional.

Practice what you preach,
preach what you believe,
and believe what is right
and righteous.

A passionate heart
committed to a clear vision
can accomplish the
impossible.

You must first have joy in your heart before you can experience peace in your life.

The wise spread their wings and embrace the winds of change.

Catch a dream and live it!

The greatest thief in our life is the one we allow to steal our joy.

Peace: **P**ray **E**veryday
And **C**herish **E**veryone

Yesterday is history.
Tomorrow is a mystery.
Today is a gift. That's why
it's called the present!

PICK PARTNERS WILLING TO SOAR WITH YOU.

Ph.D.: **Poor Hungry and Driven**

The winds of change will blow you away or take you to new heights.

"The sky is the daily bread
of the eyes."
—Ralph Waldo Emerson

The majesty of a snowfall
begins with the beauty of
an individual snowflake.

Settle for nothing less than
your best.

"If I had to single out one
element in my life that has
made a difference for me,
it would be a passion to
compete."
—Sam Walton

"If we did all the things we are capable of doing, we would literally astound ourselves."
—Thomas Edison

The attitude you embrace is more important than the circumstances you will face.

Filter all thoughts through
your heart before they
become words.

A true champion sustains
a superior performance
even when he or she
doesn't feel "100 percent."

THE ROAD TO EXCELLENCE HAS LITTLE TRAFFIC.

The rush of adrenaline is
worth the risk.

Practice while others are
sleeping.

"Work is love made
visible."
–Kahlil Gibran

Be careful: The pursuit of "perfection" can mean missing the big picture.

Success is measured in the achievement of specific goals, not in the number of hours or days spent getting there.